traveller homes

'traveller dave' fawcett

AMBERLEY PUBLISHING

First published 2012

Amberley Publishing
The Hill, Stroud
Gloucestershire, GL5 4EP

www.amberley-books.com

Copyright © Dave Fawcett, 2012

The right of Dave Fawcett to be identified as the
Author of this work has been asserted in accordance
with the Copyrights, Designs and Patents Act 1988.

ISBN 978 1 4456 0423 7

British Library Cataloguing in Publication Data.
A catalogue record for this book is available from
the British Library.

Typeset in 9.5pt on 12pt Celeste.
Typesetting by Amberley Publishing.
Printed in the UK.

Introduction

The adoption by those of us known by many names but commonly referred to as the 'New Travellers' of buses and coaches retired from PSV service arose from the emergence of the commercial and free festival scene in the late 1960s and its development during the 1970s.

This led to many deciding to follow an itinerant lifestyle, at least during the summer months, which meant that various types of transport were adopted, including horse-drawn wagons, small vans and ex-passenger service vehicles. The latter had also been commonly adapted for mobile accommodation by the UK's fairground families in the 1950s and 1960s and were often available cheaply, either direct from coach and bus firms, or via auctions, specialised dealers and scrapyards.

Interior arrangements were often basic to start with; most of the original seats having been removed, a platform for the bed was often built across the rear end, a wood burner installed and a rudimentary kitchen fitted. Further refinements depended on the owner's needs, family size, skills, and of course what could be found in industrial skips!

The same applies to the exterior appearance, often initially left in the previous owner's colour scheme, but also often repainted with flamboyant colours or with an artistic landscape scene, for example, by some of the talented mobile artists to be found within the travelling community.

Structural alterations could mean anything from the panelling over of some or all of the side windows, to creating open rear platforms (or top decks) or the addition of a second-level bedroom by attaching a small van body to the roof!

As well as providing transport for the owner(s) and their children, many homes were also used to transport various domestic animals, often just cats and dogs for company, but also goats, hens, ducks, geese and sometimes horses.

Until the mid to late 1970s, converted vehicles were still relatively uncommon at such events as the summer solstice celebrations at Stonehenge, the Glastonbury Festival and on the regional circuits such as the 'Albion Fayres' in East Anglia, and so media reportage and political police intervention remained relatively low-key.

But this situation changed in the early 1980s when folks decided to head for the Greenham Common Airbase to support the women's blockade there in a convoy of about 120 vehicles after the end of the 1981 Stonehenge Festival, which lead to the police attempting to set up roadblocks around the base and the participants being dubbed 'The Peace Convoy' by the press.

By 1982–4, as Travellers' numbers increased, partly due to the effects of the Thatcher government's economic and social policies encouraging the young inner city poor to seek an alternative means of survival, so did confrontation with regional police forces.

Conflict also arose between some members of the 'convoy' and the organisers of certain festivals who found themselves swamped by folks not prepared to leave immediately after the weekend event had finished, so creating problems for their licence obligations.

By 1984 the Stonehenge Free Festival had grown to an often chaotic event attended by over 65,000 people which lasted nearly six weeks and it was inevitable that official reaction would follow.

The first episode of mass arrest and vandalism of New Travellers' homes took place at Nostell Priory in Yorkshire after an August bank holiday, the police force motivated by their experience in combating the national miners' strike. But the most notorious police operation occurred in Wiltshire the following 1 June, during which some 500 people were detained and numerous homes deliberately destroyed – it has become known as the 'Battle of the Beanfield'.

This was followed up in 1986 by a dawn operation at Stoney Cross airfield in Hampshire, resulting in the impounding of 140 vehicles deemed to be 'non-roadworthy' as the Conservative government sought to finally 'decommission' the Convoy, who had by now acquired the media tag of 'Medieval Brigands'.

The result of these events and the new Public Order Act, which restricted the number of vehicles legally allowed in one place to twelve, led to many folks deciding to take their converted homes abroad, preferring the greater space available in southern Europe. Meanwhile, others retreated to plots of land, became boat owners or went back into brick housing.

However, the free festival scene continued to be active in the late 1980s, as more youngsters searched for something better than the low-paid urban misery created by successive Conservative governments. A new element was introduced by the move of the emerging 'Dance House' music culture from urban warehouses to open-air 'Free Party' events from 1989 onwards.

But this also created new tensions with the authorities and after the Castlemoreton Festival in May 1992 (attended by 20,000+) the response was the 1994 Criminal Justice Act (CJA). The resulting restrictions this put on the festival/party scene and daily life for the New Travellers means that the numbers of people now living in converted buses and trucks has severely declined and the days of seeing convoys of 'colourful ramshackle buses' clogging up England's country roads in the summer months are long gone.

The following selection of converted bus and coach photographs is taken from the author's personal archives and tries to show the diverse range of makes and models used as 'mobile homes', mainly from the period 1988–96. Information concerning the type of vehicle and the original PSV operator is noted, and where known names of its Traveller owner(s), followed by an indication of its current status.

HLX 403 – AEC Regent III Park Royal H30/26R – 1948 – London Transport RT586
18.9.1989 Travellers School Bus Benefit, Clyro Court, Powys
Roger's double-decker had previously been the children's play-bus at The Three Crowns pub. When the rear platform rotted, a ladder was needed to reach the upper storey and the leaking roof was repaired with gaffer tape. It is last known to have been dismantled by a preservationist in the mid-1990s and offered for sale in this condition.

XMR 231A – AEC Regent V Park Royal H41/32RD – 1956 – Cottrell, Mitcheldean (SDF 281)
28.6.1990 Glastonbury Festival, Pilton, Somerset
This vehicle, Phil's double-decker, was later scrapped.

XWV 612A – AEC Regent V East Lancs H33/28R – 1961 – Eastbourne 57 (HJK 157)
7.9.1993 Offchurch disused railway line site, Warks
John and Ceryn's bus was previously owned by Darren. It is currently used by a Dutch
company for hire as a hospitality and wedding vehicle.

MLL 722 – AEC Regal IV Park Royal RDP37C – 1952 – BEA Heathrow 1080
6.7.1991 Rutland Free Festival, Harringworth, Northants
Demo and Mandy's bus was severely vandalised during open-air storage while waiting to
be preserved, so it is due to provide parts for MLL 735, another of the five of these coaches
owned by Travellers at one time.

AAB 503A – AEC Reliance 4MU3RA Plaxton Embassy I C51F – 1962 – Shipley, Ashton-under-Lyne (30 YTC)
21.2.1992 Clifton Hall site, Clifton Campville, Staffs
Chinese Paul and Dawn's vehicle, which had previously served as a car transporter. It was later scrapped.

824 BWN – AEC Reliance 2MU3RA – Harrington Cavalier C37F – 1962 – South Wales Transport 1047
19.6.1991 Summer Solstice Free Festival, Rats Run, Longstock, Hants
Angus sold his coach for preservation in 2002 and it is now part of the South Wales Transport Collection.

XCJ 700 – AEC Reliance 2MU3RV – Duple Britannia C41F – 1961 – Yeomans, Canon Pyon
2.7.1991 Newham Drove site, Matlock, Derbyshire
This coach had been bought by Mamma Lou from a Derbyshire scrapyard. When this photo was taken, it was being lived in by Bev and Jono; it was later owned by Nicky and then scrapped.

Q295 YRX – AEC Reliance MU3RV – Duple Britannia C43F – 1956 – Lloyd, Nuneaton (VAC 640)
18.9.1989 Travellers School Bus Benefit, Clyro Court, Powys
Originally owned by Henry, then Penny, here it was in Ray's ownership. In 1995 it was sold to Wacton's Coaches to be scrapped.

OCF 222 – AEC Reliance 2MU3RA – Duple Britannia C41C – 1960 – Mulleys Motorways, Ixworth 58
20.9.1989 Hay Bluff, Hay-on-Wye, Powys
Bought out of service by Kendrix, this vehicle is here being used by Ian and Ali. Jaffa was born in it in 1995, and it might still survive.

MTG 172 – AEC Regal IV – Burlingham Seagull C41C – 1953 – Thomas, Port Talbot
15.7.1991 Morton Lighthouse Free Festival, Merseyside
This coach, here owned by Scott and Di, was later sold to John and has been stored in a barn by a collector for several years.

OST 502 (re-registered LVS 175) – AEC Reliance 2MU3RV – Alexander C41F – 1960 – Highland B24

29.5.1989 Inglestone Common Free Festival, Avon

Chris's coach had originally been converted by a naval engineer. It later travelled around Ireland in Wendy's hands before its final Traveller owners left it in a yard there, from where the Scottish Vintage Bus Museum rescued it for restoration to its original PSV condition..

BGS 705A – AEC Reliance MU3RV – MCW B40F – 1955 – Aldershot and District 273 (MOR 604)

3.8.1991 Llanbister Common Free Festival, Powys

This bus is currently used by Justin as a mobile cinema unit at festivals.

KBV 778 – AEC Reliance MU3RV – Plaxton Consort C41C – 1958 – Batty Holt, Blackburn
24.5.1992 Castlemorton Free Festival, Gloucs
Steelie and Tracy's home passed through several hands including Chris, then Dave and Annie before being sold for preservation in 2011 after a few years' storage in a barn.

948 MTD – AEC Reliance 2MU3RV – Plaxton Panorama C41F – 1960 – Monks, Leigh
26.7.1989 Treworgey Tree Fayre, Liskeard, Cornwall
Liam's coach had only been fitted with a basic kitchen here, as its main purpose was to transport four tepees. It was later scrapped.

ECK 508E – AEC Reliance 2MU4RA – Plaxton Panorama I C41F – 1967 – Premier, Preston
13.3.1994 Welham Lane site, Great Bowden, Leics
Steve's home, with its rear windows panelled over. It may have been later scrapped.

TRO 704E – AEC Reliance 6MU3R – Plaxton Panorama I C41F – 1967 – Frames, London WC1 148
29.8.1988 Ribblehead Mushroom Festival, Ingleton N. Yorks
The 'Social Bus', which was notorious for the quantities of Special Brew consumed by its many inhabitants. It was later scrapped.

KUP 201J – AEC Reliance 6MU3R – Plaxton Derwent II DP51F – 1970 – Gillett, Quarrington Hill

20.3.1989 Spring Equinox Celebration, Stonehenge, Wilts

'AEC John' is seen here sorting out his batteries, which due to alternator problems led to him needing a push-start from obliging neighbours at festivals and on at least one occasion from passing policemen! This vehicle was later scrapped after being owned by Ethen.

PEX 176K – AEC Swift 3MP2R – Willowbook B43D – 1972 – Great Yarmouth 76

8.7.1996 Festival Eurokapean, Belfort, France

The 'Slug Bus', previously owned by Twigg and Donna, was being used by Beamie as part of the Total Resistance Sound System in Europe. It was later scrapped in Spain.

JPA 85V – Albion Victor FT39AN – Heaver B35F – 1954 – Guernsey Motors 52 (6442)
29.5.1989 Inglestone Common Festival, Avon
Annie & Boysie's bus; an earlier owner had copied the JPA registration from Guernsey
8226. It still survives with Nick, but is now suffering from severe rot to the wooden frame
(especially its rear end) after years of open-air storage.

**4076 (re-registered Q147 OST, then RFO 829) – Albion Victor FT39AN – Heaver B35F – 1956
– Guernsey Motors 75**
13.1.1992 Odstone Drove site, Leics
At the time of this photo, this was Dominick's home. After being taken around Europe,
it was sold to Luke before the 12 Tribes sect used it around UK festivals and it currently
resides in Belgium with a wedding hire and hospitality company.

2616 – Albion Victor FT39AN – Heaver B35F – 1956 – Guernsey Railway 57
5.3.1992 Clifton Hall site, Clifton Campville, Staffs
Pat bought his bus from the collection of J. C. Young in Nottingham, but the poor condition of the engine meant that it had to be towed from site to site, ending up on the notorious A46 lay-by. It was last noted in 2008 in a Lydney yard, falsely registered as JPA 85V!

732 (re-registered OFF 605) – Albion FT3AB – Reading B36F – 1950 – Watson, St Martin
14.5.1993 Barrowden Lane site, Ketton, Leics
Another vehicle from J. C. Young's collection, for which Adam and Lee struggled to find a replacement EN286 engine in good condition, requiring other Travellers (including the author) to tow it around for nearly a year. It was later reduced to just a chassis-cab by a Scottish collector.

12725 – Albion NS3AN – Reading B31F – 1963 – Guernsey Motors 93
14.4.1991 Pitton site, Salisbury, Wilts
Kev still has his bus, although engine problems led to an attachment being permanently fitted through the hole in the front panel to assist during towing operations from site to site.

5708HZ – Albion Viking VK41L – MH Cars B44F – 1966 – County Tyrone Education Board
6.4.1995 Villa Nova De Poiares, Portugal
Lyle and Kirstie's home is seen having its front door repaired here outside Fran and Aide's house. They also had to replace the original Leyland O.370 engine with a Spanish version. It was later scrapped.

Above and below: **UCS 644 – Albion Lowlander LRI – Alexander H40/31F – 1963 – Western SMT, Kilmarnock CN1780**

2.11.1995 Foire Extraordinaire, Arvigna, Ariège, France

Sold to Perry by Gary and Dianne, this bus was used as part of the Hazzard Circus as it travelled around southern Europe. The day-glow nearside paint-job was carried out by Bas during the foire, but the whole vehicle is now in the more subdued red of Western SMT and is used as part of Perry's French retro-camping business.

XRL 732A – Austin K8/CVC – Reading C??C – 1955 – NBTS, Sutton (VPH 998)
20.9.1989 Hay Bluff, Hay-on-Wye, Powys
Tall Chris somehow managed to squeeze himself into this small-cabbed mini-coach, later owned by Gastro Gary and scrapped on the A46 lay-by site.

DSU 272 – Austin K8/CVC – Kenex C14F – 1951 – Margate & District Motor Services (NKT 206)
29.5.1989 Inglestone Common Free Festival, Avon
Dan's mini-coach had seen most of its side windows replaced by plywood sheeting for some reason. Later repainted black with a red, gold and green radiator grill while in Cath's ownership, it failed to find a buyer when she advertised it in the vintage press in the early 1990s and so ended up being scrapped.

VMK 200 – Bedford OB – Duple Vista C29F – 1951 – Grosvenor, Enfield
26.5.1991 Sodbury Common Free Festival, Avon
This OB had been painted red and black when owned by Carl. With Tony it was usually seen covered by a tarpaulin to prevent rain penetrating through its roof panels. It is now stored for preservation.

UYK 961 – Bedford C4Z1 – Dennis B30F – 1959 – LCC/GLC School Bus 3039
13.6.1989 Glastonbury Festival, Pilton, Somerset
John's bus had at some stage been transplanted onto an RL 4x4 chassis and was given a molly-croft roof to provide extra internal headroom. After being stored in Norfolk, he repainted it as an AFS crew-bus; it is now with a collector following his death.

BCD 933B – Bedford C4Z2 – Duple Vista C29F – 1958 – Crouch End Luxury Coaches, London N8 (42PMT)
20.3.1989 Spring Equinox Celebration, Stonehenge, Wilts
Previously owned by Mik-Mik, it is unclear who was using it at the time of this photo. It was later scrapped.

568 BYA – Bedford C4Z2 – Duple Vista C29F – 1958 – Blagdon Lioness, Blagdon
25.6.1991 Summer Solstice Free Festival, Rats Run, Longstock, Hants
Neil and Becky's home – they had bought it from Liam, who found it in a rough condition in 1989. It was last known to be with Paul in Wales, but was then seen on a farm near Lydney a few years ago.

WXE 298 – Bedford C5Z1 – Duple Midland B30F – 1960 – Ministry of Aviation
11.8.1991 Trecastle Free Festival, Powys
Pete is seen here about to enter his and Sarah's bus, which was later owned by Terry before ending up as a child's bedroom in Spain with Skippy and Jane.

UBL 690 – Bedford C5Z1 – Duple Midland B30F – 1960 – AWRE, Aldermaston
8.7.1996 Eurokapean Festival, Belfort, France
To provide more space for his family Baz decided to cut his bus in half and lengthen the chassis. Unfortunately, before this could be completed the Dutch site it was parked on was evicted and the authorities scrapped it.

CHA 875Y – Bedford J2SZ2 – Willowbrook B19F – 1972 – MoD (RN) (04RN00)
4.8.1991 Llanbister Common Free Festival, Powys
Ownership details for this vehicle are unknown to the author. It was later scrapped.

BTK 2C – Bedford J2SZ10 – Duple Midland Compact C19F – 1965 – Dortax, Dorchester
1.8.1989 Treworgey Tree Fayre, Liskeard, Cornwall
Jim Blim's smart-looking 'blim' bus. It was later scrapped.

JPN 110D – Bedford J2SZ10 – Duple Midland Compact C19F – 1966 – Bletchley Self Drive, Bletchley

22.6.1989 Glastonbury Festival, Pilton, Somerset

This was Jezz and Mare's home before it was sold to Jim and Vicky in 1991. It was later scrapped.

LPN 735E – Bedford J2SZ10 – Duple Midland Compact C19F – 1967 – Setterfield, Milford Haven

19.6.1992 Sewerage Farm site, Donnington Le Heath, Leics

Liz's mini-coach seen here in the early stages of being converted. It was later scrapped.

FEG 887K – Bedford J2SZ10 – Plaxton Embassy C20F – 1972 – Shaw, Maxey
7.5.1995 St Y Bar Free Festival, Ariège, France
Mike spent several years travelling around Europe with Bek in his bus before parking it on his land in Brittany.

ABD 699A – Bd J2SZ10 – Plaxton Consort V C20F – 1963 – Kirkham, Church (6579 TF)
3.8.1991 Llanbister Common Free Festival, Powys
Tilly and Craig were using their home to sell food and drink to festival goers. It was later scrapped.

3037 WY – Bedford J2SZ7 – Plaxton Consort III C18F – 1961 – Grange, Yeadon
20.6.1990 Glastonbury Festival, Pilton, Somerset
James and Loll's 'Twilight Zone' mini-coach.

3037 WY – Bedford J2SZ7 – Plaxton Consort III C18F – 1961 – Grange Yeadon
27.5.1991 Sodbury Common Free Festival, Avon
James and Loll had added a Commer Space Van to create an upstairs bedroom. It was later
scrapped.

14223 (re-registered JFL 93D) – Bedford J4EZ1 – Reading B35F – 1966 – Guernsey Motors 99

7.7.1993 Barrowden Lane, Ketton, Leics

Bought by Matty and Sylvia from J. C. Young's collection, this bus was later stored at Shobden and then bought by Janice, and has recently been re-sprayed in green and red.

AAB 695A – Bedford J4LZ1 – Duple Midland B30F – 1961 – Salopia, Whitchurch 144 (WNT 244)

28.8.1995 Aurillac Street Theatre Festival, Cantal, France

Previously owned by Ady, at the time of this photograph it was Shaun's. He'd added an Austin FX4 taxi as a bedroom; the next owner removed this and painted the vehicle silver. It was later scrapped.

LRM 829L – Bedford J3LZ7 – Strachan B23F – 1962 – MoD (RN) (21RN59)
10.6.1989 Rats Run, Longstock, Hants
Andy is seen here juggling outside his and Nikki's home, later owned by Nathalie. It was later scrapped.

UDG 924 – Bedford SB3 – Duple Vega C41F – 1958 – Silvey, Epney
18.9.1989 Travellers School Bus Benefit, Clyro Court, Powys
This bus was previously owned by Jano in the mid-1980s but it is unknown who owned it at the time of this photograph. It was later scrapped.

AFE 218A – Bedford SBG – Burlingham Seagull C34F – 1954 – Wing, Sleaford 2 (HCT 990)
14.7.1991 Morton Lighthouse Free Festival, Merseyside
Simon and Clare's stylish home was later owned by Rupert and Claire, then Slim. It currently survives in Devon.

329 FPE – Bedford SB8 – Burlingham Seagull C41F – 1958 – Ben Stanley, Hersham
20.6.1990 Glastonbury Festival, Pilton, Somerset
Seen here as part of the Croissant Neuf Circus, this bus was later neglected in an Oxford yard by a collector before being rescued by Alan for further use as a home and regularly driven between England and Spain.

SJN 885 – Bedford SB8 – Harrington Crusader C41F – 1959 – Nicholls, Southend
26.5.1991 Sodbury Common Free Festival, Avon
For some reason, an AEC badge had been fixed to the front of Crusty Pat's SB8. This vehicle was later scrapped.

PVO 945 – Bedford SBG – Duple (Fishmouth) Vega C36F – 1954 – Kenworthy, Hoyland Common
18.6.1988 Summer Solstice Celebrations, Cholderton Lay-by, Wilts
Kate and Walter's unusual Duple-style coach with a sign advertising 'Egg Butty's' for sale among the plants on its dashboard. Walter started to repair the wooden body structure some years ago, but it is still sitting in a barn, waiting to be finished.

997 XXN – Bedford SB5 – Duple Northern Firefly C41F – 1964 – Barton, Chilwell 997
5.5.1991 Hungerford Common Free Festival, Hungerford, Berks
A coach that had been in Travellers' hands since the early 1980s is here being used by John
and Ceryn. It was later scrapped.

299 DWU – Bedford SB5 – Duple Northern Firefly C41F – 1963 – Longster, Pateley Bridge
27.5.1991 Sodbury Common Free Festival, Avon
One of very few Firefly-bodied Bedfords to survive; it is still with Ed and Jenny in
Brittany.

Above and below: POO 32D – Bedford SB5 – Duple Bella Vega C41F – 1966 – Boon, Boreham

21.6.1989 Treworgey Tree Festival, Liskeard, Cornwall

Tat and Bridget's home, one of only four vehicles allowed to drive away from the 'decommissioning' of the Convoy at Stoney Cross in 1986.

12.11.1989 Market Bosworth, Leics

Tat was well known for being manic in keeping the interior spotless, something which became a more difficult task when they later had children! Although its current status is unknown, it might have been seen on a Devon farm in 2003.

DAP 190C – Bedford SB3 – Duple Bella Vega C41F – 1965 – Evan Evans, WC1
8.7.1996 Eurokapean Festival, Belfort, France
Originally bought out of PSV service by Bex in Cornwall, at the time of this photograph it was being lived in by Nick and Nikki. It is thought to have been scrapped by now.

BCF 547C – Bd SB5 – Duple Bella Vega C41F – 1965 – Combs, Ixworth
31.8.1989 Havens Free Festival, Amsterdam, the Netherlands
The 'Six o'Clock Bus' is seen here resorting to a tarpaulin to try and keep some of the damp Dutch weather away from leaking skylights. It was later scrapped.

Above and below: OVW 687D – Bedford SB5 – Duple Bella Vega C41F – 1966 – Supreme, Hadleigh, Essex
9.6.1989 Rats Run, Longstock, Hants
Alan's 'Landscape Bus' with one of Bas's 'all-over' bus murals. It was later scrapped.

FRO 266C – Bedford SB13 – Duple Bella Vega C41F – 1965 – Simmonds, Letchworth
10.9.1989 Rougham Harvest Fayre, Suffolk
Phil and Sheris's home had a raised bedroom, perhaps due to their coach having served as a car or bike transporter at one time. It was later scrapped at the Hempnall Airfield site, and the remains were sold to Jordan's scrapyard.

MMC 307C – Bedford SB5 – Duple Bella Vega C41F – 1965 – RACS, London SE18 K0177
26.7.1989 Treworgey Tree Fayre, Liskeard, Cornwall
After changing their engine for the third time, Dave and Jo decided it was easier to change vehicles, so during the festival their home was systematically dismantled by Dave and HB and all the parts were sold to other Bedford owners on site to pay towards their next home, a Duple Bella Vista.

Q915 GJA – Bedford SB5 – Duple Bella Vega C41F – 1963 – Watson, Dundee (J 10857, OTS 836)

26.8.1991 Twistleton Dale Free Festival, N. Yorks

Charlie's coach is seen here still displaying the company name of its last PSV operator, Tantivy, based in Jersey. It was later scrapped.

AOR 212B – Bedford SB5 – Duple Bella Vega C41F – 1964 – Whittle, Highley 14 (3405 NT)

31.3.1994 Dommet Wood site, Somerset

Guy's home had already seen several owners and changes in colour, a steel grill replacing a broken windscreen at one stage. He then painted it red before touring around Europe. It was later scrapped.

HNP 814J – Bedford SB5 – Duple Vega 31 C39F – 1971 – JMT 32 (J 29627)
24.8.1996 Aurillac Street Theatre Festival, Cantal, France
At the time of this photograph, it was being used by an English street theatre group. It was seen advertised for sale in 2009 by its French then-owners for €10,000.

GFO 494K – Bedford SB5 – Duple Vega 31 C41F – 1972 – Owen, Knighton
8.7.1993 Barrowden Lane site, Ketton, Leics
'Comfy Lux' Nick's home, whose rear end had previously been shorted by several inches after a Traveller's coach following behind on a downhill journey suffered brake failure, leaving the owner no choice but to use Nick's coach to stop his! It was later scrapped.

Above and below: NUX 186G – Bedford SB5 – Duple Midland B42F – 1968 – Shropshire CC
12.12.1989 Norton-Juxta-Twycross green lane site, Leics
Steve and Sue spent a winter gradually insulating the bus interior with cork tiles, suited to the curved roof lines. It was later sold to a friend thinking of setting up a health farm in Ireland, so it could perhaps still survive there.

XHR 508A – Bedford SB3 – Duple Vega C41F – 1960 – Premier, Watford (9042 AR)
22.6.1991 Summer Solstice Free Festival, Rats Run, Longstock, Hants
This coach had been driven to the 1989 Treworgey Tree Fayre by Womble, who swapped it for a Morris Commercial with Jim, who lived in it with Becks, before selling it on to Tim and Zippy. Tim is currently rebuilding the wooden body structure.

WLB 490 (re-registered AJU 773A) – Bedford SB1 – Duple Vega C41F – 1959 – Essex Pride, Rainham
23.7.1989 Treworgey Tree Fayre, Liskeard, Cornwall
'Wilberforce' is seen here coated in the notorious diseased 'Treworgey dust' which, like the throat infections it caused, lingered long after the end of the festival. It was later scrapped.

558 FBF – Bedford SB3 – Duple Super Vega C41F – 1962 – Happy Times, Wednesfield
11.8.1991 Trecastle Free Festival, Powys
Julian, Alison and Dan's home, which they bought after a car had wrecked their Bristol MW5G. They replaced its original Bedford 300 petrol engine with a Leyland O.350 diesel. It is now being restored to PSV condition by its current owner.

YRV 140 – Bedford SB5 – Duple Super Vega C41F – 1962 – Byng, Portsmouth
19.6.1990 Glastonbury Festival, Pilton, Somerset
Previously owned by Dawn and Ady, at the time of this photograph, it was Celia and Ritchie's, then bought by Tara. By 2012, only the chassis-cab survives as a source of spare parts for other surviving Super Vegas.

24 HTO (re-registered YSY 296) – Bedford SB1 – Duple Vega C41F – 1960 – Skill, Nottingham

FEX 13 (re-registered GSK 378) – Bedford SB3 – Duple Super Vega C41F – 1961 – Yaxley & Sayers, Great Yarmouth

3.9.1991 Mallerstang Free Festival, Kirkby Stephen, Cumbria

'Milli-com' had a succession of owners from the mid-1980s, including John, Missey, Paula and Don; here it was with Karlos and Adie, and finally Karen, who transplanted its engine into 456 HYC, a Super Vega, in 1994.

FEX 13 also passed through a few hands, including Matt and then Karlos, before eventually being scrapped.

WBD 777 – Bedford SB8 – Duple Vega C41F – 1960 – Canning, Kings Sutton

17.6.1991 Stockbridge Down, Hants

'Team Yorkshire Pudding' (the name of its previous owners, a racing team) is seen here being given an ill-omened 'flame' paint-job by Karlos; it was burnt out only a month later in a candle fire after being sold to Chris at the Morton Lighthouse free festival on Merseyside.

Above and below: YET 500 (re-registered XMR 812A) – Bedford SB3 – Duple Super Vega
C41F – 1961 – Riley, Rotherham
28.5.1991 Sodbury Common Free Festival, Avon
Mike and Sharon's coach had previously been transformed for the owner of its last PSV
operator, Abingdon Coaches, to transport a horse and carriage. It was later sold to Tony and
then to Iain, before ending up stored on a farm in Devon and scrapped in 2004.

647 ACE (re-registered OSJ 293) – Bedford SB5 – Plaxton Embassy I C41F – 1961 – Harvey, Cambridge 43
10.9.1989 Rougham Harvest Fayre, Suffolk
Johnny's Embassy is seen here looking very smart. It was later owned by Jason and maybe others before being scrapped.

550 6RK – Bedford SB8 – Plaxton Embassy I C41F – 1962 – Bennett, Croydon 6
30.10.1989 Market Bosworth site, Leics
During the 1980s this coach was owned by Ritchie, with an eye-catching colour scheme. As can be seen here, Little Nick preferred the traditional Traveller's combination of red and green; he later sold it to Pete and Maria when returning to being house-drawn. Its current status unknown. It was last taxed in 1991.

URU 980 (2448 MN when used on the Isle of Man) – Bedford SB3 – Plaxton Consort C41F – 1957 – Excelsior, Bournemouth

26.5.1990 Inglestone Common Free Festival, Avon

When it had been 'Petrol Bus Dave's' coach, it was another of the four homes allowed to drive away from Stoney Cross in 1986; here it was 'Rob The Light's', and was later burnt out in a candle fire when parked on site at Pitton in 1991.

EBW 62B – Bedford SB13 – Plaxton Embassy III C41F – 1964 – Don, Southsea (653 GBU)

22.3.1992 Clifton Hall site, Clifton Campville, Staffs

This was Paul's home, which later passed to Spencer, who then sold it to another Traveller in 2011.

POT 506G – Bedford SB5 – Plaxton Panorama II C41F – 1969 – Durrant, Alford
26.5.1990 Inglestone Common Free Festival, Avon
Clare's coach had an appropriate registration for a Traveller. It was later scrapped.

JWW 646J – Bedford SB5 – Plaxton Panorama C41F – 1971 – Baddeley Bros., Holmfirth 108
8.7.1993 Barrowden Lane site, Ketton, Leics
Freeno, Sharon and Soma's home, which had to be scrapped in the mid-1990s in Portugal after being vandalised.

GPA 77J – Bedford SB5 – Plaxton Panorama C41F – 1971 – Bicknell, Godalming
26.8.1995 Aurillac Street Theatre Festival, Cantal, France
Irene still uses her home around the UK festivals; it is currently painted mid-blue.

XBW 718H – Bedford SB5 – Plaxton Panorama C41F – 1970 – Smith, Upper Heyford
9.7.1995 Eurokapean Festival, Belfort, France
Head and Laurie later sold their home to Nigel and Rachel and their three lads; it was last heard of being used as a static caravan by a German traveller in southern Spain.

Q205 ATV – Bedford SB3 – Strachan B39F – 1967 – MoD (RAF) (40AC16)
3.9.1991 Mallerstang Free Festival, Kirkby Stephen, Cumbria
Ownership details for this bus are unknown, but presumably it has been scrapped by now,
last having been taxed in 1992.

WDV 176S – Bedford SB5 – Strachan B36F – 1966 – MoD (RN) (52RN36)
26.5.1990 Inglestone Common Free Festival, Avon
'Blunderbus' is seen here showing signs of the rust associated with Strachan's steel bus
body. It is still in use, but now in Portugal, where the dryer climate and lack of winter road
salt will help stop any further deterioration.

GHX 271B (Fictive) – Bedford VAS – Strachan SC B-F – 1972 – LB Lewisham (MLB 115L or MLB 117L)
6.1.1995 Ellie's Land, Villa Nova Do Poaires, Portugal
Neil and Dave's bus had acquired the registration from another vehicle when it was recovered from a squat in Bilbao. It was later burnt out in a forest fire at Casa Da Val in Portugal in 2000.

UDL 6K – Bedford SB5 – Strachan SC B45F – 1972 – IoW CC
15.6.1989 Glastonbury Festival, Pilton, Somerset
Ownership details for this bus are unknown, but it was later scrapped.

YUL 159H – Bedford VAM3 – Willowbrook B-D – 1970 – GLC Supplies Department 1019
9.6.1989 Rats Run, Longstock, Hants
'Petrol Bus John's' home had previously served as a thirty-two-seater mobile classroom for the ILEA. It was scrapped after the 1990 Glastonbury Festival.

UNL 237H – Bedford VAM70 – Willowbrook DP45F – 1970 – Raisbeck, Bedlington
7.6.1992 Charity Farm site, Breedon, Leics
Fred and Ness's home; I seem to recall that it had to be parked on a slight slope in wintertime for their water heater to function correctly. It was later scrapped.

GPW 414D – Bedford VAM5 – Duple Bella Venture C45F – 1966 – Carley, Fakenham
29.8.1988 Ribblehead Free Festival, Ingleton, North Yorks
Ron's coach 'Windblown' was very appropriately named for this site next to the famous Blea Moor railway viaduct during this festival. It was later scrapped.

FNT 900D – Bedford VAM5 – Duple Northern Viscount C45F – 1966 – Corvedale, Ludlow 32
10.2.1992 Clifton Hall site, Clifton Campville, Staffs.
Sarah's home, with Julian's Celtic decoration. It is seen here for sale, as she had decided that it was time for a change of lifestyle. It was later scrapped.

KDV 477F – Bedford VAM14 – Duple Viceroy C45F – 1967 – Geen, South Molton
28.8.1995 Aurillac Street Theatre Festival, Cantal, France
Gary and his family's home is seen here missing one part of its split windscreen for some
reason. Its current status is unknown.

UDF 615H – Bedford VAM70 – Duple Viceroy C45F – 1970 – Warner, Tewkesbury
28.8.1995 Aurillac Street Theatre Festival, Cantal, France
Mike's Viceroy is tatted down and ready to leave the festival's camp site before armed CRS
officers started to get heavy-handed. It was later scrapped.

JWF 35E – Bedford VAM14 – Plaxton Panorama I C45F – 1967 – Boddy, Bridlington
27.5.1991 Sodbury Common Free Festival, Avon
Kissy's home looks as if her then-toddler daughter had been crayoning on the side of it! It
was later sold to Gareth, who took it to Europe, where it was eventually scrapped.

MNW 710F – Bedford VAM70 – Plaxton Panorama I C45F – 1968 – Kitchin, Leeds
6.4.1990 Green Desert's HQ, Kilin Farm, Rougham, Suffolk
Glenda's coach is no longer roadworthy, but still serves as a guest bedroom in Wales.

XEL 332B – Bedford VAS1 – Plaxton Embassy II C29F – 1964 – Corvedale, Ludlow 20 (3819 NT)
28.4.1989 Beltane Free Festival, Swindon, Wilts
This is a home which also functioned as a festival café. However, police action meant that service here had to be suspended until the event was relocated below the Uffington White Horse the next day. It was later scrapped.

DUD 702C – Bedford VAS1 – Plaxton Embassy IV C29F – 1965 – Smith, Upper Heyford
2.3.1992 Clifton Hall site, Clifton Campville, Staffs
The previous ownership of this bus is unknown, but at the time of this photograph it was Brin's, later being sold to Becks in Somerset before being scrapped.

VMA 466E – Bedford VAS1 – Plaxton Embassy C29F – 1967 – Bostock, Congleton 2
7.9.1993 Offchurch disused railway site, Warks
'Chester Bus' was bought out of PSV service by Nigel and Rachel. Here, Hagar Tom was explaining how its rear window came to be broken thanks to a low-flying pot of mayonnaise, which led the next owners, Laurie and Alan, to build a bedroom 'extension' in its place. It was later owned by Ollie and is now thought to be in Cornwall with its current occupiers.

DHN 455C – Bedford VAS1 – Plaxton Embassy C33F – 1965 – Alpha, Brighton
1.3.1991 Wash Common site, Newbury, Berks
Richard's home was one of eight VAS1 chassis to be extended from the usual seating capacity of twenty-nine. It is thought to have been scrapped in the Oxford area in the mid-1990s.

53

CYC 942C – Bedford VAS1 – Duple Bella Vista C29F – 1965 – Baker, Weston-super-Mare 59
1.8.1993 Butts Quarry Rave Party, Derbyshire
The ownership and current status of this bus are unknown.

AWX 153G – Bedford VAS5 – Duple Vista 25 C29F – 1969 – Greaves, Bingley
21.6.1991 Summer Solstice Free Festival, Rats Run, Longstock, Hants
Beryl's 'The Flying Shuttle' is now painted green and stored on her land in Wales.

LLE 791P – Bedford VAS5 – Dormobile B31F – 1976 – LB Enfield 9807
23.6.1994 Cumeille Commune, St Hilare, Aude, France
Triggy had sold his bus, seen here with another example of Julian's Celtic knotwork paint-jobs, to a French Traveller (one of the 'Shanka Tribe'), which was a common practice during the 1990s.

TLM 443R – Bedford VAS5 – Wadham Stringer B29F – 1977 – LB Enfield 9932
7.7.1996 Eurokapean Festival, Belfort, France
Bez brought his home across the Channel for this festival. However, no information has come to light about its subsequent history.

VAX 839H – Bedford VAS5 – Duple Vista 25 C29F – 1970 – Davies, Tredegar
29.4.1989 Beltane Free Festival, Swindon
The 'Bluebell Bus', so called from the artwork of Sherwin, who had been its previous owner. At the time of this photograph it was Sioux and Steve's. However, by 1991 the rear springs were suffering from the weight of the Rayburn used for heating and cooking, and the bodywork from age, so Sioux decided to transplant its engine into another Duple Vista and the rest was left for scrap on a site at Pil.

OVB 189F – Bedford VAS5 – Strachan Pacerider B21FL – 1968 – LB Haringey 9492

18.2.1995 Coimbra, Portugal

Paddy and Emma's home had been fitted with a non-standard windscreen due to damage caused by a JCB during an illegal eviction while travelling in the UK. It was later scrapped, although OVB 187F from the same fleet still survives.

DLL 536J – Bedford VAS5 – Strachan Pacerider DP26F – 1971 – Autotours, London, SW5
4.10.1990 The Trump site, Michaelchurch Escley, Herefordshire
Taisa's bus was later scrapped, but at least two similar vehicles still survive in Travellers' hands.

DLG 651F – Bedford VAS5 – Plaxton Panorama II C29F – 1968 – Lingley's Sale Away, Sale
16.6.1990 Barton Stacey Airfield Free Festival, Hants
The ownership and later history of this vehicle are unknown to the author. It was last road legal in 1990.

CWX 431H – Bedford VAS5 – Willowbrook B30F – 1970 – Hargreaves, Bramham
3.9.1991 Mallerstang Free Festival, Kirkby Steven, Cumbria
Another bus that had passed to a Scout troop after its PSV service days were ended before becoming a mobile home. It was later seen by the author, painted blue and black, in Portugal during the winter of 1994/5. It has presumably been scrapped by now, unless perhaps it is still parked up somewhere in Europe?

EMM 456J – Bedford VAS2 – Willowbrook B25F – 1971 – Metropolitan Police 3338G
8.7.1996 Eurokapean Festival, Belfort, France
Along with Scout troops, ex-police buses are also popular with New Travellers! Here 'Pink Sue' and Mickey's bus had acquired an Atkinson radiator grill in place of the original Willowbrook one. It is currently painted a more subdued colour in the UK.

JGY 952K – Bedford VAS2 – Willowbrook B25F – 1971 – Metropolitan Police 3355G
23.9.1989 Autumn Equinox Celebration, Stonehenge, Wilts
Another bus from the 'Met', here being used by Danny, who had replaced the original bumper with one from a TK with extra spotlights. It is parked next to an ex-Western National Bristol MW5G and an ex-MOD RL. It was later scrapped.

VOT 563T – Bedford VAS5 – Wadham Stringer B23FL – 1979 – Cleveland SS
26.5.1990 Inglestone Common Free Festival, Avon
Roseanne's home is seen here. It was later scrapped.

CNV 20K – Bedford VAS5 – Plaxton Panorama III – 1972 – KW Coaches, Daventry, A97
26.5.1991 Sodbury Common Free Festival, Avon
Mike and Sharon's coach, which was later scrapped, is seen here parked next to the ex-ICI
SB3-Coventry Steel Caravans JUR 994C used for some years as the New Travellers' 'Skool
Bus' (deliberate misspelling).

LYJ 483P – Bedford VAS5 – Duple Dominant C29F – 1976 – Marsh, Plumpton
3.9.1995 Pierre's Land, Carlucet, Lot, France
This Dominant looks to have served as a racing car transporter prior to being bought by
a Traveller.

DEX 22C – Bedford VAL14 – Plaxton Panorama C52F – 1965 – Seagull, Great Yarmouth
14.2.1994 Barrowden Lane site, Ketton, Leics
The Traveller history of this vehicle is unknown to the author. It was later scrapped.

EUG 911D – Bedford VAL14 – Plaxton Panorama C49F – 1966 – Kitchin, Pudsey
10.7.1993 Barrowden Lane site, Ketton, Leics
Mike and Cookie's coach is seen here being prepared for repainting before going to Europe.
It was later scrapped by Danny on a site in Telford.

MPR 532H – Bedford VAL70 – Plaxton Panorama Elite C53F – 1970 – Rendell, Parkstone
7.1.1990 Gopsall Wharf site, Snarestone, Leics
HB's coach is seen in the January mist. It is now more of a static home for him and Bas's superb dragon mural has faded after years of exposure to the English sun.

HDL 231E – Bedford VAL14 – Duple Northern Viceroy 36 C52F – 1967 – Southern Vectis 409
18.6.1991 Stockbridge Down site, Hants
Gavin's 'Free Party People' coach, ready to move on after police had served an eviction notice at 8 a.m. It was later owned by Michelle, who painted it red and had it driven to the Castlemoreton festival in 1992 by Ray. It was later noted as parked in Moseley in the mid-1990s and then scrapped.

DRM 561K – Bedford VAL70 – Duple Viceroy 37 C53F – 1972 – Stephenson, Maryport
19.9.1993 Old Oundle Road site, Wansford, Cambs
Ian is seen here changing a rear wheel on his coach, which was practical for his and
Michelle's family at the time, but they soon decided to sell it and become horse-drawn! It
was later scrapped.

AJA 132B – Bedford VAL14 – Strachan B52F – 1964 – North Western Road Car 132
13.9.1989 Park Vale Road, Highfield, Leicester
Nick lived in his bus for ten years, as part of Snap Dragon Circus, but scrapped it after
failing to find a buyer in 1994.

1542 DH (Re-registered EBW 936A, then PFF 802) – Bedford VAL14 – Plaxton Val C52F – 1963 – Dawson, Walsall
28.5.1991 Sodbury Common Free Festival, Avon
Tom and Cherie's home is seen here being used to sell duty free alcohol and tobacco at the festival. It later went with Martin and Kisey as PFF 802 to Europe, where it was the victim of a candle fire at Pierre's land near Carlucet, France, in 1996.

AJU 670B – Bedford VAL14 – Duple Vega Major C52F – 1964 – Boyden, Castle Donington
28.5.1991 Sodbury Common Free Festival, Avon
The ownership details for this vehicle are unknown to the author. It was later scrapped.

HGM 615N – Bedford YRQ – Marshall B42D – 1975 – AWRE, Aldermaston
12.2.1991 West Down Common site, Hants
Steve's home is one of several buses used by the nuclear bomb factory to end up with the 'Peace Convoy'! It is still in use by someone as a mobile home and is regularly seen at UK festivals.

DFU 95L – Bedford YRQ – Willowbrook DP45F – 1972 – Millard, Brigg
3.8.1991 Llanbister Common Free Festival, Powys
The ownership details for this vehicle are unknown to the author. It has presumably now been scrapped, last having been taxed in 1993.

XRO 344M – Bedford YRT – Plaxton Panorama Elite III C53F – 1974 – Smith, Rickmansworth

25.6.1991 Summer Solstice Free Festival, Rats Run, Longstock, Hants

Johnny is seen sat at the wheel of his coach, waiting for the council to finish laying gravel so he can drive off what had been a 'green lane' until the typical English summer weather turned it into a muddy track. The coach was later owned by Keld, who had the misfortune to park it at the rat-infested Chiseldon Firs site, where it was burnt out after Traditional Travellers threw fireworks through the cat-flap. The remains passed to Gemini Travel, Bishops Stortford, for spares.

HOR 324L – Bedford YRQ – Duple Viceroy C45F – 1972 – Browning, Box

31.3.1994 Dommet Wood site, Chard, Somerset

Astral's coach, which she sold to Fleur to finance trekking in India. It was scrapped by a later owner.

JDG 782N – Bedford YRT – Duple Dominant C53F – 1975 – Perrett, Shipton Oliffe
24.5.1999 Mons La Trivalle, Hérault, France
This was Nigel and Rachel's home for their three lads, dogs, cats, mice … It was scrapped in 2001 on a farm at Segonzac, France.

LVS 441P – Bedford YRT – Duple Dominant C53F – 1976 – Armchair Coaches, Brentford
28.9.1997 Montauban, Tarn and Garonne, France
Little Tat's home, which shared my apple-picking park-up for a while. It was later scrapped.

431 FHW – Bristol LD6G – ECW H33/25RD – 1959 – Bristol L8541
9.4.1999 Vale De Vide, Portugal
Shaun's double-decker is listed in the *Guinness Book of Records* after completing
a round-the-world tour with previous owners in 1988–9. From 2000–10 it seems
to have been parked in Woodbridge, Suffolk, where its condition deteriorated,
but hopefully Mark, the current owner, will be able to restore it to a roadworthy
condition.

4386 LJ – Bristol FS6G – ECW H33/27RD – 1962 – Hants and Dorset 1463
24.8.1996 Aurillac Street Theatre Festival, Cantal, France
Sprocket Circus's home, which has also visited many countries over the years:
India, Pakistan, Australia, North and South America. Now they travel mainly
around southern France and Italy.

CHT 541C – Bristol FLF6B – ECW H38/32F – 1965 – Bristol C7198
26.5.1990 Inglestone Common Free Festival, Avon
Colin's double-decker looks as if it has just delivered its fare-paying passengers to this festival. He built a recording studio as well as living space inside it. It is currently painted red and under the ownership of a wedding and hospitality hire company in Kapellen, Belgium.

197 KFM – Bristol SC4LK – ECW C33F – 1959 – Crosville CSG636
10.6.1989 Rats Run, Longstock, Hants.
Bugsy is seen starting up the coach he shared with Hannah at the time; it would have found it difficult to pass current emission testing for PSVs! It was later scrapped.

351 EDV – Bristol SUL4A – ECW B36F – 1961 – Western National 637
23.9.1989 Autumn Equinox Celebration, Stonehenge, Wilts
This bus has been a travelling home since 1983, although it has not moved from a side street in Brighton for several years now. At the time of this photograph it was Dave Stooke's, and then it passed through several owners, including Colin, Glen and Mark. It is currently with Josh.

EDV 531D – Bristol SUL4A – ECW B36F – 1966 – Western National 676
12.6.1989 Penton Mewsey Free Festival, Andover, Hants.
Another surviving SUL4A that has been in Travellers' hands since 1979, and Pierre's home since the mid-1980s.

BHU 972C – Bristol MW5G – ECW B45F – 1965 – Bristol 2604
2.1.1992 Clifton Hall site, Clifton Campville, Staffs
Blah Dave was refitting his bus's interior after recently buying it from Paul and Jane, who had acquired it from Nicky. Then, in 1992, it suffered from the widespread flooding of southern France while Dave was parked near Rennes Le Bains, but it later became mobile again for a few years when used by Mark and his family in Europe.

BLV 654A – Bristol MW6G – ECW C39F – 1961 – Lincolnshire Road Car 2818 (RFE 461)
24.9.1991 Allen Knot Quarry site, Troutbeck, Cumbria
Helen and Kerry's home, later sold to other Travellers when they returned to being 'house-drawn'. Its current status is unknown but it was last taxed in 1992.

Above and below: **268 KTA (31915 Guernsey Rwy 153) – Bristol SUL4A – ECW C33F – 1962 – Western National 418**

6.5.1993 Kelham Bridge Farm, Ibstock, Leics

Jane's coach was another acquired from J. C. Young's collection. The interior was still being fitted out when these photographs were taken. It was later owned by Rebecca before a collector scrapped it in 2006.

SPK 117M – Bristol LHS6L – ECW B35F – 1973 – London Country BL17
25.8.1995 Aurillac Street Theatre Festival, Cantal, France
Lizzy's home, which she named 'Phoebus Apollo', later had fish scales painted on its sides.
Its current status is unknown, but it has probably been scrapped.

GLJ 481N – Bristol LH6L – ECW B43F – 1974 – Hants and Dorset 3549
2.7.1991 Newhaven Drove site, Matlock, Derbyshire
Marion and John's home, which they were gradually painting dark green when this
photograph was taken. It is now used by Vicky and Iain in Portugal, where it survived a
forest fire at Val Da Casa in 2000.

LNN 94K – Bristol RELH6G – ECW DP47F – 1972 – East Midland C94
13.6.1989 Glastonbury Festival, Pilton, Somerset
Marek's home was last seen at a Rainbow Camp in 1990. It was later scrapped.

EHW 314K – Bristol RELH6G – Plaxton Panorama Elite II C47F – 1972 – Bristol 2162
5.5.1991 Hungerford Common Free Festival, Berks
This was Andy and Elaine's home for their three children, but later the same year it was the victim of a candle fire.

UXD 308L – Commer VCAW 887 – Rootes B??D – 1973 – Luton BC 5973
12.6.1988 Calleva Free Festival, Aldermaston, Berks
Phil's ex-airport passenger shuttle bus, prior to having its exterior transformed by Bas and Steve.

27.5.1989 Inglestone Common Free Festival, Avon
Phil arriving with Subtle Steve and Bas's artwork, guaranteed to cause a second glance from passing motorists. It was later scrapped by its next owner.

PKG 535H – Daimler CRG6LX – Willowbrook H44/30D – 1969 – Cardiff 535
28.5.1995 Aurillac Street Theatre Festival, Cantal, France
'Crow Bar', which toured around Europe's rave scene with its occupants in the mid-1990s.
Its current status is unknown, but it has probably been scrapped by now.

NFA 14M – Daimler CRG6LX – Willowbrook H44/34F – 1973 – Burton 14
9.6.1990 Penton Mewsey Free Festival, Andover
Alex had only recently acquired this double-decker with its appropriate NFA registration, so its interior had yet to be converted when this photograph was taken. It was later scrapped.

Above and below: **696** YTD – **Ford 570E** – **Duple Yeoman C41F** – **1962** – **Morecambe Motors**

5.5.1991 Hungerford Free Festival, Berks

A coach which had previously been used as a BRISCA stock car transporter until Ben purchased it in the late 1980s. Seen here in Bez and Gog's ownership, the rear doors had been replaced with a fixed window and boot, but they had not managed to find a correct front bumper for it. Later stored by Gog, it passed to a preservationist in 2000.

JOO 987 – Ford 570E – Plaxton Embassy I C41F – 1962 – Verrall and Freeman, Loughton
27.6.2000 Mons La Trivalle, Hérault, France
The home of Martin and Sarah, along with their sons Jeddah and Bobbo. It is now sat, immobilised and unused, in the French Alps.

FRE 967A – Ford 570E – Plaxton Embassy II C41F – 1963 – Finchley Coaches, Finchley N20 (2 JNM)
21.10.1992 'The Redhouse' site, Parwich, Derbyshire
Andy and Charlie's coach had previously been converted into a horse transporter, resulting in the rear roof section being raised and turned round and a wooden door-ramp inserted. It was later scrapped.

VFN 549 – Ford 570E – Duple Midland B42F – 1960 – Wren, Canterbury
14.4.1991 Pitton site, Salisbury, Wilts
Earlier owned by Mark, this vehicle was sold to Bugsy for £100. It was later vandalised at its current storage location.

TMD 424S – Ford R1014 – Wadham Stringer DP45F – 1977 – LB Redbridge
21.12.1989 Winter Solstice Celebration, Stonehenge, Wilts
Katie and Simon's home, which was later painted red, gold and green with Julian's Celtic knotwork designs before being burnt out in London.

COA 467C – Ford 570E – Duple Trooper C41F – 1965 – Worthington, Birmingham
4.8.1989 Treworgey Tree Fayre, Liskeard, Cornwall
Alan and Sam's coach with its roof covered in the infamous Treworgey toxic dust. It was later scrapped.

DRE 203E – Ford R192 – Duple Empress C45F – 1967 – Greatrex, Stafford 132
23.6.1991 Summer Solstice Festival, Rats Run, Longstock, Hants
This vehicle was home for 'Jolly Jay' and his family for many years. It was later scrapped.

DLB 469J – Ford R192 – Plaxton Panorama Elite II C45F – 1971 – Dix, Dagenham
21.8.1992 Rod's Farm, Sheepy Magna, Leics
This coach had earlier been converted by a showman and was said to have weighed 12 tons.
Its subsequent history is unknown.

OTM 522H – Ford R192 – Duple Viceroy C45F – 1970 – Thorne, London SW2
8.5.1990 Gopsall Wharf site, Snareston, Leics
Kate is seen here reversing out of the lane leading to a disused canal wharf that had served
as a winter site for a dozen homes. The coach had previously owned by Janet and Glen. It
was later scrapped.

MED 394P – Ford R1114 – Duple Dominant C53F – 1976 – Smith, Wigan 19
15.12.1993 Northborough, Cambs
Dave and his partner were due to be evicted soon after this photo was taken as the landowner didn't have planning permission for them. The vehicle is thought to have been later scrapped.

CBA 187L – Ford R226 – Duple Dominant C53F – 1973 – Fieldsend, Salford
29.8.1989 Havens Festival, Amsterdam, the Netherlands
This coach had ended up being absorbed into a two-storey bar and stage construction at this long-term squat. However, it was later scrapped when the Dutch authorities eventually evicted the site.

BRY 950C – Ford 568E – Marshall B42F – 1965 – Leicester CC
13.9.1989 Park Vale Road, Highfields, Leicester
Schmitt's bus, which has been a static caravan on a Corby transit site for many years now.

KMP 684P – Ford R1014 – Marshall B45C – 1975 – L.B. Waltham Forest 3320
26.5.1990 Inglestone Common Free Festival, Avon
This vehicle was bought to serve as a tour bus for the RDF group, but it soon became a home for ex-band members Fred and Luap and was treated to another of Bas's bus mural paint-jobs. In 1991 it was sold to Sarah and Skwid for their family, but was severely vandalised while they were parked alone in a lay-by near Loughborough in 1992 and scrapped.

HTG 506D – Ford R192 – Strachan Pacesaver II B46F – 1966 – Bebb, Llantwit Fardre
27.3.1994 Smeeton Westerby site, Leics
The bus had recently been bought by Claire and Jonathan from the nearby Errington's Bus Company at Oadby. It was later sold onto other Travellers when they became house-drawn in Wales. Presumably it has now been scrapped.

TBV 249K – Ford R226 – Caetano Estoril C53F – 1972 – Ribblesdale, Blackburn 49
24.3.1992 Clifton Hall site, Clifton Campville, Staffs
Gavin's stylish home, appropriately already painted in the colours of the Anarchist flag. He soon sold it to Sarah and Skwid to replace their vandalised R1014 bus and it was later scrapped.

PTH 225R – Ford A0610 – Wadham Stringer B??FL – 1977 – West Glamorgan CC
27.5.1989 Gordano Services, M5, Bristol
'The Henge Hopper' en route to Inglestone Common Free Festival. It was later known to have been on the A38 Fraggle Rock site in Cornwall, waiting to be restored by its then-owner.

UWB 189S – Ford A0609 – Asco Clubman C18DL – 1978 – Leon, Finningley 93
1.11.1994 Villa Nova Do Ciera, Portugal
Mick and Immy's home is seen here parked up outside Adam's barn conversion. It was scrapped later the same year.

3716 ED – Leyland PD2/40 – East Lancs H37/28R – 1962 – Warrington 88
11.9.1989 Rougham, Suffolk
Tony and Gizz's home had needed to have its roof cut off while travelling in Europe with Hazzard Circus in the 1980s as it was the only way to comply with the height restriction for Switzerland's road tunnels! Tony has now repainted it red.

479 CFJ – Leyland PD2A/30 – Massey H31/26R – 1961 – Exeter 79
29.5.1989 Inglestone Common Free Festival, Avon
Lin and her family had arrived in a convoy at the police roadblock designed to prevent access to this festival site at the same time as a second convoy arrived from the opposite direction, so the police gave up! Her bus, which had been painted by Bamboo, another well-known travelling vehicle artist, is currently sat in her son's barn awaiting restoration.

WFY 48 – Leyland PD2/40 – Weymann H37/27F – 1962 – Southport 48
15.6.1992 Tony Goodwin's Yard, Carlton, Yorks
Ribs bought this double-decker which had been shortened to 24 feet for recovery usage by Merseyside PTE, repainted it and fitted out the interior. It was subsequently owned by Terry, with whom it now sits, engineless, on a transit site in Corby.

BHN 740B – Leyland PD3A/1 – Metro-Cammell H41/33R – 1961 – Leicester Corporation 246 (246AJF)
20.9.1992 Upton Drove site, Hinckley, Leics
Graham and Annie had also bought their home from a Carlton yard, Joe Sykes' PSV Sales. They later swapped it with Jonathan and Claire for their Ford R1114; it was later taken to Normandy, where it was swapped for a tractor and box-trailer. It then sat on Roy's farm at Ceauce until a new landowner decided it was a safety risk to his children and scrapped it.

232 CRV – Leyland PDR1/1 – Metro-Cammell H43/33F – 1963 – Portsmouth 232
17.9.1989 Traveller's Skool Benefit, Clyro Court, Powys
Adam's eye-catching Atlantean, which he travelled around Europe in as part of the Mutoid
Waste Company. It had previously been used as a campaign bus by Greenpeace.

OWJ 169A – Leyland PSUC1/1 – Alexander DP41F – 1962 – Trent 182 (YRC 182)
19.6.1990 Glastonbury Festival, Pilton, Somerset
The owners' history for this vehicle is unknown.

LFM 329 – Leyland PS1/1 – Weymann B35F – 1950 – Crosville KA253
12.4.2004 Olonzac, Hérault, France
This bus was originally taken around southern Europe by Syd and later swapped for a boat with Stewart. It was stored for sometime in the Aude region then parked outside a tyre depot before being returned to the UK to be restored.

176 DCD – Leyland PSU3/3R – Plaxton Panorama C49F – 1964 – Southdown 1176
5.5.1991 Hungerford Common Free Festival, Berks
Zoe's home is seen here with an appropriate slogan, 'Freedom On Wheels', from a previous owner, the National Street Van Association. It has presumably been scrapped by now and was last taxed in 1999.

VWG 401 – Leyland PSUC1/12 – Alexander Y C41F – 1963 – Alexander Midland MPD261
22.3.1991 West Bridgford Cemetery site, Notts
When this photograph was taken, this was Shaun's home. It was then owned by Tim and Sian, and later scrapped.

NDN 665M – Leyland 850TR – Sparshatt B31F – 1973 – British Rail
26.8.1990 The Trump, Michaelchurch Escley, Herefordshire
At the time of this photograph, this bus was used by Cath and her family. Its later history is unknown.

WCW 193M – Leyland 550FG – Lex Tillotson C21FL – 1973 – Salford Education Dept.
20.3.1991 Lasham Airfield site, Alton, Berks
Adrian's austere-looking Lex Tillotson-bodied home is seen here. It was later scrapped.

KAE 290L – Leyland 420FG – Longwell Green B11FL – 1972 – Avon CC
21.6.1991 Summer Solstice Festival, Rats Run, Longstock, Hants
Whoever the owner of this taxed FG bus was liked their house plants! The original sliding door and fixed window have been replaced with more practical wooden ones in this picture. It was later scrapped.

PNP 66L – Leyland 550FG – MacLay Wayfarer C24F – 1972 – Darke, Evesham
5.6.1993 Strawberry Fayre, Cambridge
Rob had just repainted his home. It has recently been bought by Crispian, after being stored unused for several years.

MHM 296P – Leyland 350FG – Dormobile B17FL – 1976 – GLC ILEA A1750
6.7.1991 Rutland Free Festival, Harringworth, Leics
Clive's 'Out To Lunch' FG mini-bus had earlier been used as roadside snack bar.

GWX 840J – Seddon Pennine 4 – Pennine DP45F – 1971 – Edwards, Liverpool
2.8.1991 Llanbister Common Free Festival, Powys
The ownership history of this vehicle is unknown to the author. It was later scrapped.

XVU 343M – Seddon Pennine 4 – Seddon B23F – 1973 – SELNEC 1713
24.3.1992 Clifton Hall site, Clifton Campville, Staffs.
Another Seddon, for which I've no Traveller history recorded.

About the Author

After graduating from Leicester University in 1984 with an Honours Degree in Archaeology, Dave found the Free Festival scene more fulfilling than the one proposed by the academic world, so after several years of travelling during the summer months he adopted the bender lifestyle, then bought an ex-British Telecom Bedford TK at an auction before finally acquiring a licence to drive it.

Deciding something larger was more suited to his needs, a 1966 Albion Chieftain furniture lorry was bought in 1992 from Arthur Fossett, a Midlands Showman who'd used it as a mobile 'shooting gallery' for twenty years.

But the prospect of trying to live with the restrictions imposed by the 1994 Criminal Justice Act (CJA) led to the decision being made to abandon the UK. Now surviving as an itinerant fruit picker in France during the summer months, where the minimum wage removes the need to depend on state benefits over the winter period.

Author's Notes

My photographic record of converted trucks and buses formed the basis for the Traveller Homes website I created to record this segment of English social history that's still struggling to survive, although, as mentioned in the Introduction, on a much smaller scale than had been seen during the 1980s and 1990s.

Information about the owners of the vehicles comes from my own and other travellers' memories, so apologies for any mistakes, and I hope no offence has been caused to those whose names have been omitted, or to those who would preferred not to have been mentioned!

Corrections and additions to photo captions and additional images are always welcome via my website: www.travellerhomes.co.uk

Acknowledgements

To ensure that the original PSV operator and chassis information is correct, and for his proofreading, the author is grateful for the help received from Martin Ingles.

For information about surviving Bedford buses: John Wakefield's www.wakefieldfiles.co.uk

For information concerning Bristol Buses: Rob Sly http://bcv.robsly.com

For information concerning AEC PSVs: www.busweb.co.uk/aecbus/

For information concerning PSVs in general: www.buslistsontheweb.co.uk